AF430216

LUBUÑA DIMUREI

The Garifuna Alphabet

By Sheryl DeVaney

Illustrated by TullipStudio

To the heartbeats of the Garifuna community,

This alphabet book is not just about letters; it embodies a culture
shaped by our ancestors' dreams and our children's aspirations.

For every Garifuna child learning their language and
the elders safeguarding it: may this book ignite our heritage in
young hearts and highlight the beauty of our distinct voice.

PABLO LAMBEY
FOUNDATION

Aa   garünati

Agütü

Grandmother

01

Bb

ba

Baruru

Plantain

Cc

cha

Charigi

Grapefruit

Dd

da

Duna

Water

Ee

Egi

Grater

Ff

fa

Fanidira

Flag

Gg

ga

Gabayu

Horse

Hh

ha

Halaü

Chair

Ii

Idibu

Tree

Kk

ka

Karu

Car

10

Ll la

Lefan

Elephant

Mm
ma
Mansana
Apple

Nefu

Nine

Ñn ña

Ñulú

Soft

Oo

Ounli

Dog

Pp

pa

Punta

Garifuna dance

Rr

Ra

Rin

Rice

17

Sabadu

Shoes

Tt

ta

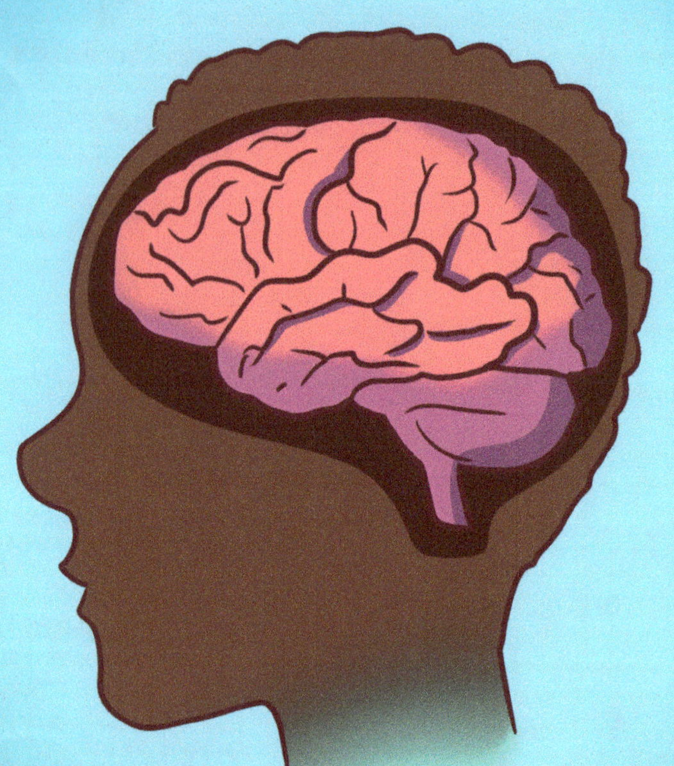

Tutenu

Brain

19

Uu

Ubóu

World

Üü

Üdüraü

Fish

Ww

Weyu

Sun

Yy

ya

Yalifu

Pelican

About the Author:

Sheryl DeVaney, acclaimed author of the Garifuna alphabet book, hails from the lively town of Dangriga, Belize. Beyond her literary pursuits, she's a dedicated wife, devoted mother, and the visionary founder of the Pablo Lambey Foundation.

Sheryl's connection to the Garifuna culture is deeply personal, shaped by the wisdom and teachings of her grandparents, Pablo and Alice Lambey. Their influence and the community's rich traditions ignited Sheryl's profound appreciation for her heritage.

Driven by her passion for safeguarding the Garifuna language and traditions, Sheryl penned the Garifuna alphabet book. It transcends being merely a language resource; it's a heartfelt invitation into the soul of the Garifuna community.

The Pablo Lambey Foundation, a tribute to her grandfather's legacy, pledges to channel this book's proceeds toward its mission. Through her literary and philanthropic endeavors, Sheryl aims to inspire others to embrace their heritage, ensuring that these rich traditions are passed down and cherished by future generations.

www.ingramcontent.com/pod-product-compliance
Lightning Source LLC
Chambersburg PA
CBHW061147160726
48006CB00038B/2300